How Not To Be An Asshole

How Not To Be An Asshole:

21st century life lessons for those with their heads up their asses

by

E. B. Davis II

TWO CAT PRESS

Somerset 163 Ltd
P O Box 82382
Columbus OH 43202

First edition published May 1, 2016
Copyright © 2016 by Somerset 163 Ltd

Copyright allows creators to create without fear, promotes free speech and
brings color to the world. Thank you for buying an authorized copy of this book
and for not stealing it or its contents from the author.

ISBN-13: 978-0692707296 (Two Cat Press)

ISBN-10: 0692707298

Printed in the United States of America
10 9 8 7 6 5 4 3 2 1

This is where a pithy quote would go.

I don't have one.

Deal with it.

How Not To Be An Asshole

Lesson 1: You're Not That Interesting

Stop giving a shit what people think of you. It doesn't matter anyway. People are rarely thinking about you. There is a lot of attention given to people who don't deserve it and that makes it seem that everyone is looking at everyone all the time, judging, whispering, gossiping. These things do happen but not as often as you think. If you want to be the center of attention, then do something worth watching. Make a difference and make it interesting. Don't just do stupid shit to get people to look at you and laugh. Do important things, hard things, things that matter and people won't be able to look away.

Stop thinking that you are the center of anyone's universe because unless you are a parent, you are not. Not your husband or wife's, not your boyfriend or girlfriend's. If you are, there are bigger problems. There is no circumstance other than being an infant where someone should be completely consumed with another person. This even goes for children. At some point, children need to know that they are not the center of the universe. This comes at about age three so up to that point, obsess away.

If your significant other has no life outside of you, that's a serious fucking problem. Run away. Fast. Don't fucking look back. No one person should be wholly and completely consumed with another person. That's just a recipe for disaster. If they don't want you to spend time with your friends away from them, if they don't want to be with your family at an event and don't want you to go do, that's a problem. If you cannot text or talk to someone on your phone without them checking your messages, or trying to inject themselves into your conversation to distract you from the other person, that's a serious fucking problem. There is no trust there. That person doesn't trust you at all. Even if you've given them zero reason to distrust you. They are not healthy and they are not healthy for you. I'm not a mental health professional but I know that shit's fucked up. If this is happening to you, get help. Somehow. Please.

Cultivate your own personality and interests and be an interesting person to be around. Michael Dell, the founder and CEO of Dell Computers, basically said something like 'Never try to be the smartest person in the room. And if you are, then I suggest you invite smarter people, or find a different room." Just replace 'smart' and 'smarter' with 'interesting' and 'more interesting'. If you are the most interesting person in the room, find a different room or invite people who are more interesting than you. If you think that you are that interesting and that everyone is watching what you are doing and you're not a YouTube sensation then you need a fucking reality check. Most of the time, no one is paying any attention and that feeling kinda sucks balls. You want people to notice you and be interested in what you are doing. Why? Is it left over from when mommy and daddy gave you a prize for taking a shit in the potty like a big kid? Is what you are doing really worth anyone spending their time on it? If not, then be more interesting or don't fucking worry about it.

If you are going to go out on a limb and try to be more interesting so that more people will look at you because you feel that is what you need to have any kind of confidence in yourself, which makes no fucking sense, then be prepared for the haters. You can't have the love without the hate. They will come and they will not be kind. If you are prepared for that, then you probably didn't need to be encouraged to be more interesting in the first place. The bottom line is don't be surprised that haters will overwhelm the admirers and don't cry when it fucking happens. Not everyone can be famous, thank goodness.

Stop trying to fit in with whatever new trend has come down the pike from some stupid ass celebrity. Let me be clear: celebrities are mostly marketing, at least the ones that are always in the magazines and tabloids. Most of the time, they are doing what they can to stay relevant. Their paycheck relies on someone buying the magazine and reading the story but the real story is that it is all probably fabricated anyway. If it isn't them getting a paycheck, someone is. Tabloid gossip is stupid shit drummed up from circumstantial situations to sell magazines. If you really want to know what a celebrity is doing that is worth reading about, then read more reputable magazines. Tabloid gossip is just another form of "bread and circuses" (See Lesson 8). It's all devised to draw your attention away from things that matter, things that might make you think on your own. Think on your own, please. For fuck's sake, think on your own.

Just do *your* thing and find your people. Find your tribe. Don't try to force people to be in your tribe if they don't want to be, it is just not fucking worth it. All non-authentic tribe members will do is try to make you miserable. If you have to convince someone to be in your life, they are not worth your fucking time. This applies to family members, too. Also consider reevaluating what you think your tribe is going to look like. If you stop overlooking the awesomeness in front of you for some stupid preconceived idea of what you think things should be like, you are going to royally miss out. That guy that maybe isn't as good looking as you think your potential boyfriend should be, maybe he'd be the best thing that ever happened to you, but no, you're too busy looking for the perfect guy that looks the perfect way. I can attest that those guys, they know they look fucking perfect and some of them use that as a weapon. Not all but most do. Same with the ladies. There might a girl who is in no way going to model for the Victoria's Secret Lingerie show but that doesn't mean they aren't the perfect fit for you. Stop judging people for how they look and instead give them credit for how they treat you. If they treat you well, keep them around. If they treat you badly, kick them to the fucking curb. It might also warrant a mention of what being treated well and badly means, see the paragraph above or check out the myriad of books on this subject at your local library.

Lesson 2: Your Knight is Shining Armor is a Fucking Lie

No one is going to rescue your ass so stop thinking that it is going to happen and start doing something to rescue your own ass. This one is mostly for the ladies. Girls, you've been indoctrinated with this idea of a knight in shining armor with all those stupid princess movies that have been churned out over the years. Have you looked around you lately? The world is fucking filled with bros and chivalry is mostly dead. It might be around here and there, like with some genuinely kind and gentlemanly roughnecks I met years ago when driving cross country and stopped in the middle of butt-fuck Texas to crash for the night. Talk about a bit of dissonance: these guys looked every bit of the word "rough neck," scary as fuck, and yet they helped me with my bags and my squirmy toddler so aside from a random run-in with some tough as nail oil workers, no one is really going to be there to catch your ass. If someone is, consider it a wonderful surprise but don't keep expecting that to happen. Otherwise, this shit's all on you. *You* have to pay your bills, *you* have to clean your house, *you* have to find yourself a job and you are entitled very little. See Point 4 to learn what you are entitled to. No man is really going to take care of all your problems and if they say they are, then you can rest assured that with that promise is going to come a whole other host of problems that will make your first set seem like a fucking walk in the park.

As for money, the lottery is a fun little game to play occasionally, it only takes ONE ticket to win. It is not a fucking retirement plan, asshole. Don't ever spend more than you can afford to lose on any kind of gambling. I like a good game as much as the next guy and I don't mind putting a little skin in the game to keep things interesting. Kenny Rogers your ass and know when to walk away. Play the lottery, the proceeds supposedly go for a good cause: the schools, but play it responsibly. Buy one ticket, not a hundred tickets. Don't fucking drop your entire paycheck on a lottery jackpot that you have a 1 in 292,201,338 of winning. Lightning can strike, it happens, people win that shit. I'm not saying it doesn't but I'll bet the vast majority of major lottery prize winners didn't dump a grand on tickets to win it.

The same thing goes for the casino, the race track or the backroom poker game. Don't fucking get in over your head. The excitement and the rush is great but it's not life. It's a game, a stupid fucking game and you don't need to ruin your life over it. If Lady Luck isn't giving you a lap dance, then get up and go home. Save your money for food, idiot, and gas to get to your job. Don't blow it on the roll of the dice, a horse with a weird name or a some poor dog who doesn't want to live in a cage 23 hours as day. Better yet, roll those scones

you're dying to spend into a retirement fund or a college account for

your kid. Make it game, bet your friends you *can't* save ten grand in

a year and the loser has to pay the winner another $500. That'll

keep your shit interesting.

Lesson 3: Bad Shit Happens Every Day. Deal With It.

Bad shit happens to good people all the time and it's not God trying to test your mettle. It's just bad fucking shit and we all go through it. If you like the idea of God and of putting your faith in something bigger than you to help you through, I think that's great. Ultimately, though, it's you who has to solve the problem. I believe in something bigger than me but I don't believe that it dictates my actions or is guiding me in any way. I think that in my DNA, cultivated over the thousands of years that humans have been around is an intrinsic guidance system provided for me by the Universe. If I feel dialed in to what is happening around me then that guidance system, call it intuition, is more accurate. If I'm checked out instead, then things are not working right, the calibration is all off and shit hits the fan. Shit just happens. It's not God's will and it's not the devil. Hand wringing and prayer might get you through the short term; it might get someone backed away from the ledge but in the end, wading through the shit is what gets someone to the other side. Diving in, facing your shit, seeking real world solutions to problems, get your fucking hands dirty and solve your shit.

The Law of Attraction is a wonderful thing. There is an element to it that I like: Like attracts Like. If you are good, doing good and being good, then good things are going to happen. Why? Because you have shifted your mindset away from looking at everything through a fucking negative filter to a positive one. You are now looking at things from the perspective of "Well, this kinda sucks balls but how can I make it better? Where's the good in this shitastic situation?" It's still a bad situation but now you are looking at it from an angle of productivity and prosperity instead of desperation and scarcity.

I get it, shit is fucking hard. When life deals you a blow to the metaphorical gonads, it's easy to curl up and vomit on the floor instead of walking that pain off. Crying in a corner or under the blankets, while trying to eat copious amounts of ice cream is so much easier that the alternative: getting up and handling the problem. Have you ever tried to eat ice cream while curled up under a blanket? That shit ain't easy and yet it seems like an easier solution than working through your problems. I think somewhere it says "God helps those who help themselves" and whereas my concept of God is iffy, I like the saying anyway because it is true. Pull yourself up by your bootstraps, dust off your hands and set about doing what needs to be done. It's all about doing the work. Are you starting to see a pattern here?

Work is what we are made for; whatever that might be at the moment. Work also helps when you are feeling helpless. Sometimes it helps to get up and clean the kitchen like a mother fucker just to feel like you are doing something productive. If you are having a panic attack at 3am like I've had, laying in bed thinking of every fucking worse case scenario is not helping. What would help is getting out of bed, finding a notepad and a pen and then cleaning something. It doesn't matter what, as long as it can be done in a quiet enough manner to not wake the rest of the damn house. Keep the pen and pad nearby because I guarantee that once you take your worried little mind off of whatever problem you think you have and start cleaning something, those answers are going to come to you. You'll want that pad and pen nearby to write down all the fucking fantastic ideas you now have to solve your problems. I'd suggest the shower but the pad and paper won't make the trip back. I tried a grease pencil once in the shower but it was a no-go. Cleaning is the next best thing for opening the mind to possibilities. While you are scrubbing away at the goo that hides under the burners on the stove, your other mind is busy throwing off the chemicals of anxiety and it, too, can get down to work. Even your brain needs to do some fucking work.

The goal here is to get wrapped up in the minutiae of cleaning and cleaning and cleaning. Don't go all OCD, just use it as a tool to clear your mind of the bullshit and let the good stuff come to the surface. The last panic attack I had resulted in me sitting down at the computer at 3 o'fuck-me-clock to write. I need to write to get the shit out. It worked. I was able to get about three and a half effortless hours of productivity out and great things started to happen. I got up and I did the work. Do the fucking work, mother fuckers. JUST DO IT. Which leads me to my next point....

Lesson 4: Lose The Entitlement Attitude, You Dumb Fucks

You are guaranteed very little so quit acting like an entitled bitch and settle in for an uphill battle. Clean water, clean air and a butt load of opportunity: that's what you can feel entitled to and if you don't get those three things, raise a big fucking stink. Nestlé shouldn't get to privatize the world's water supply, China shouldn't get to damage half the fucking planet and rich white dudes shouldn't get to take away opportunities because it might compete with their bottom line. Fight for these things because some day, they might be completely gone. As far as feeling like mommy and daddy need to provide for your every whim, get your head out of your ass. Someday, mommy and daddy are going to die and who is going to spoon feed your needs then? Are you going to find a Sugar Momma or a Sugar Daddy to take care of you? The odds of that happening are unlikely. Not impossible but unlikely. There aren't that many around and you might have to compromise more than you'd like to actually get that kind of deal...and they don't last. New models come along all the time. You'll also compromise on things like your self-worth, you dignity, your fucking mental health. By all means, if that is your retirement plan, then forge ahead. For the rest of us, with some semblance of self-worth, we're going to do what we need to do to get what we what. It's called Hustle, bitch. Learn it. Respect it. Do it. Much more on this later.

Lesson 5: Don't Be A Psycho Fuckstick

Everybody has fucking baggage and the funny thing about baggage is that it comes with you no matter where you go. Think moving to the other side of the country or world is going to magically make all your problems disappear? Here, suck on this Nope Stick because that shit will follow you no matter where you go. Your shit will always find you. It's yours. It wants to be with you and it will do anything to stay. Baggage is the ultimate stalker.

The Grass is Greener Syndrome will kill your spirits quickly. Life will not be better in Milan or to wherever you want to run away. Your new destination might be more expensive and exciting, sunnier, have new people and new stimulating things but at the end of the day when you crawl in to bed, your baggage is right there waiting for you, keeping your bed warm, ready to spoon you to until morning. "Hello. Remember me? I'm still here, Mother Fucker. Hold me." It won't go away until you acknowledge that is is there, think about where it came from and decide to do something about it.

Everyone's issues have a source. There truly are accidents and random events, I believe that, but there are also situations that keep arising because the same bad decisions keep getting made. Overall, when someone starts complaining about how their life sucks and nothing good happens and they are tired of the shit storm that is always brewing about them and it is just blah blah fucking blah all the time, that is because they cannot seem to get their head out of their ass long enough to make a good decision. Sometimes, the best decision ends up not being the best choice in the long run but at the time the choice was made, that was unknown. It is doing the best you can with what you have at that moment. If things end up not being as ideal as they could be, so be it but don't actively make shitty decisions. Taking the time to think something through before making a rash decision takes practice. My Mom always says "When in doubt, don't."

If the same bad decision keeps getting made, then there is a reason for that. I encourage you to sit your ass down and relax a bit, let your mind wander and be open to the idea of a fucking epiphany. I had one or two after I moved away from home, like far away from home....as in 2,500 miles away. They came slowly at first and I wasn't sure what the hell was happening to me but then some biggies showed up. I was laying by the shitty pool in my backyard. It was sunny, the day was warm, the dog was nearby. I was happy at that moment and contented with where I was in my life. My subconscious decided that was a good time to do a serious mic drop on me. I was free from some of the outside pressures that I grew up with. I was in a new place, with great roommates, pursuing something I really wanted. My mind was open to new possibilities, ones that I couldn't have had back home. While laying next to that shitastic pool, oh my gawd was it crappy but it was clean, filled with water, and ours, I wasn't thinking about anything in particular. I was just enjoying the lovely day, a day with no responsibilities; a day in a week with fresh, never-before options, when a little black bubble of truth floated up from my subconscious and burst itself all over my happiness. The blow of it was like being doused by a bucket of fucking ice water: it was shocking to my system. All at once, I fucking *knew*. You know how people say that they had an "ah ha!" moment? That was a fucking epic one. All of this happened inside of me. There was no dramatic gasp of breath while I sat up and looked around astounded. There was just the dog. I may have stopped petting her when the truth hit. Maybe a short hiccup in my breath. I didn't get up and run over to call someone or write it down or any of that. What was once hidden deep in my mind was now obvious. It was out. It was there and I could never un-know it.

After that first one by the pool, my mind was now poised, primed if you will, to receive more shit my brain had to tell me. I had distanced myself from some influences by moving away. Doing so allowed me to focus on other things. This shift in focus gave my brain the liberties to say "Okay, you are now ready for some truths, bitch. I'm bringing this shit. Deal with it" and I did. I dealt with it. It was like a whole new realm was open to me. Before, I was too deep in my own shit with other shit constantly being added to the shit pile to ever really dig out from it. It wasn't until I moved away and left that shit pile behind. (I ended up making a new one.) My problems followed me to the new zip code but upon arrival, once there was an entirely new energy around me, a positive one, a supportive one, my brain felt comfortable enough to say "you need to know this shit. I'm ready to get rid of some of this baggage." Once I knew the things my brain had to say didn't mean I automatically knew what to do about it. I didn't. I didn't have the tools to fix the issues that my brain had brought up. What I'm saying is that if the same situations keep happening to you, there is a fucking reason. Find a way to put yourself in a position that is different and better than the last and allow your brain to tell you why things are they way they are. There is always a fucking reason.

Time for some highbrow shit. Seneca the Stoic wrote letters of a moral sort to Lucilius. The one this quote is from is Number 17 and is on philosophy and riches, I like this because it deals with baggage. For me, this quote isn't so much about the money but about the thought processes. Here, just read this awesome shit: "I shall borrow from Epicurus: 'The acquisition of riches has been for many men, not an end, but a change, of troubles. I do not wonder. For the fault is not in the wealth, but in the mind itself. That which had made poverty a burden to us, has made riches also a burden. Just as it matters little whether you lay a sick man on a wooden or on a golden bed, for whithersoever he be moved he will carry his malady with him; so one need not care whether the diseased mind is bestowed upon riches or upon poverty. His malady goes with the man.'" Basically, your shit comes with you, bitches. If you win the lottery and you were always broke before with shitastic money management skills, the odds are pretty damn good that your are going to be broke again after blowing through how many fucking millions of dollars you won.

Unless you figure out where your shit is coming from and can address it at the source, nothing is going to fucking change. You can keep doing the same things over and over again and expect a different result, but that's just fucking crazy. Einstein said so. Look it up. In that phone I know you have in your hand right now.

Lesson 6: Know Your Shit. Own It. Fix It.

Knowing what your shit is is NOT the same as saying you fixed it. Fuck Charlie Sheen and blinking his problems away. He's a fucking whack job for more than just that. Don't be Charlie Sheen. Just because you now have a firm grasp of what your true issues are, doesn't mean that you automatically have the tools to fix those issues. Seek help. Find counsel. Get in touch with someone more knowledgeable than you who can help you gain the skills you need to fix your shit. There is no shame, EVER, in asking someone for help if they have more knowledge than you on the subject. Most people genuinely want to help others, some do it for free, others ask for a fee commensurate with their level of expertise. Do not fear paying for what you need. Get mommy and daddy to foot the bill this time then cut the fucking cord. Find someone who has this knowledge and make sure it is someone you jive with. Don't settle for the first schmuck Google lists because you don't want to do any more work to find something perfect. Take the time to find the right person to help you work on your shit. This is important work and you need to find the right person. Should I say that again? Are you listening? Is your fucking nose stuck in your phone, endlessly scrolling through shit that doesn't matter? Are you even paying attention to anything? Again, find someone who you can work with at the price you can pay and put the fucking phone down after you've called them to make an appointment and be prepared to do some serious fucking work. More than anything else, working on yourself is some of the most important shit you can do. It is now time to parent yourself. Winning!

This is going to be some of the hardest shit you'll ever do. You'll have to face all of the bad stuff about yourself. The good thing is that you don't have to take anything personally. Put it in perspective: if you didn't know before, you're about to know now and knowing is half the battle. Just ask GI-Joe. Seriously. If things are sucky as hell and you need help to fix the issues, then put your fucking pride away, check that shit at the door of your therapist's office. Don't worry, you can have it back later. Settle in for some lessons in reality and get your homework assignment. You have to be willing to change and change takes work. You also have to be willing to acknowledge that you're probably an asshole on some level and not being an asshole, which has come so easily for you, is going to take work and time.

Lesson 7: How Not To Be a Dumbass Parent

Parenting is fucking relentless. Making babies isn't hard. It's quite fun. Gestating a baby and extruding it into the world...all of these are simple acts. Parenting it, on the other hand, is a fucking ultra-marathon of epic proportions. Keeping a child alive is not difficult. If you are able in anyway to be dialed in to another human being, to be aware of their body language and communication style, to put the needs of someone else ahead of your own for awhile, you'll find that babies are not difficult to sustain. You feed them well, (you don't give a baby soda and Doritos, asshole), clothe them (thrift store shit is fine), make sure they sleep (regularly, when you decide they should sleep, not when the little fuckers collapse from a sugar crash and pure exhaustion), keep them from danger (as in, don't fucking take a nap with your two year old awake who just learned how to unlock the door. They'll be dead in the street or the neighbor's pool because your ass is fucking stupid), provide for their mental stimulation (and I don't mean endless TV and video games. Take them out in the world, to the zoo, the library, to the fucking park to feed the damn ducks, let their little asses get chased by a hormonal goose)... but parenting them? Guiding them through the world to be good people? Teaching them everything from how to use a fucking fork to wiping their own ass to how to make a good decision and how to regulate their emotional life?... That's fucking endless. Those kids you see that are fucking heathens? Who bully other kids? The ones who have no fucking manners? Those parents have checked out of parenting and have left the kid to figure it out on their own. Some kids do and turn out fine, and some don't and they end up in prison. There may be many reasons for this. Maybe those parents are working 60+ hours a week to pay the bills, maybe there is no family around to help out so the kids are with a sitter who has very little vested interest in doing more than making sure the heathens stay alive. I get it. Parenting fucking sucks ass sometimes. It never ends. The goal of any parent is to do a good enough job to be 99.5% obsolete by the time the child is an adult. The age at which this child is officially an adult varies from child to child despite what the government says. Eighteen is still pretty young. Many people don't remove their heads from their assess until well in to their 20s, some into their 30s.

Mommy and daddy need to get to a point where they no longer need to provide for the child's every need. Parents have to cut the cord at some point. There needs to be a point of no return in many ways. I'm not saying that parents should be all "Fuck you, Junior. You're on your own!" If there is a genuine need for help and the parents can provide it to an adult child without the child taking the parents for granted or with an understanding that they won't continue to save their ass, then by all means, do so. If the child is just an adult baby, calling mommy and daddy for every little thing that comes up, then no. Figure out your own shit, Junior. Don't expect mommy and daddy to buy you a fridge full of groceries because you spent your paycheck on hookers and blow. Do not expect them to bail your ass out of jail because you were stupid enough to get a DUI and do not expect them to call up your teacher and argue about a grade you received because you felt it wasn't necessary to do any actual fucking work. Suck it up. Do the fucking work.

Normal, functioning people who contribute to society do not rely on mommy and daddy to take care of their problems. They grab their problems by the horns and tackle that shit to the ground, hog tie it and prep it for the spit. I'm serious. I'm tired of stories of kids who got pissed they didn't get an A on a term paper because they did nothing to deserve it or some asshat who didn't get promoted and their mommy calls the boss. What the fuck is that? Is that real? Does that happen? My parents were all like, "What did you do wrong? How did you fuck that up?" The parents of kids like that, they checked out of parenting. They couldn't stand to see their kids cry, or be upset with them. "I'm not your fucking friend, I'm your parent. That's the way this is going down. This is not a democracy. You can voice your opinion, child, and you can make your argument and I have every right to veto that shit down." There is nothing wrong with allowing the child to make an argument. My kid negotiates with me all the time. Sometimes the argument is valid and I agree, other times I agree and veto anyway and then explain why. Regardless, I do not care that my child is pissed at me or my decision making. Learn to tolerate disappointment, child. Keep your expectations low and then you'll be pleasantly surprised.

Lesson 8: Leave Wallowing in Shit to Pigs

Don't wallow in your own shit because shit stinks and other people can smell it. If you don't seem to have any friends, if you are not getting invited out to parties and it seems that everyone else is doing things without you then check yourself. Are you complaining too much? Do you endlessly talk about yourself and your shitty problems? Do you make shit up to sound like everything is fucking Kardashian grand when it's really Honey Boo Boo bad? People can usually see through that shit and will stop wanting to hang out with you so stop it. We all have problems, baby, you ain't the only one. If you want to talk things through with a trusted friend, that's great. Buy them lunch, ask to bounce a few things off of them and see what they say. If all you want is a friendly shoulder to cry on, that's fine, too, just make sure you stipulate that at the start of the conversation. It is perfectly okay to say, "Can I vent for a moment?" or "I just need to word vomit all over the place, is that okay?" When people know what they are in for, they are better able to prepare for it, even if they only have two seconds to do so.

Pro Tip: if you are a woman and you are talking to a male friend and don't say you just want to vent, more than likely he will try to solve your problem. If you are a man and you do this to a female friend, this might be okay. If you are a woman and you do this to another woman, they will probably respond with agreement and affirmative nodding as if to say,"Right on, sister." It is okay to ask for what you need from either gender. If you want advice, ask for it and be prepared to take it. If you don't take it or try to fix the situation and you are still complaining, don't ask for advice from that person again about the same problem. That person will just think "I gave you advice, you didn't even try it, I'm not giving you anymore." If you say you just want to vent, then no advice need be given. Don't vent too often about the same thing. The point here is that you need to work on your shit. Get dirty and do the work. Need a new job? Fucking find one, and I get it, finding another job IS a fucking job. Don't have a degree? Figure out how to get one if that's what you need. There are resources and ways of doing things that might not be ideal for the short term but can get the shit done. Nothing is going to be perfect. On the other hand, don't be that guy that is always on top of the world. People see right through that shit, too. Normal people have problems and it is okay to mention them from time to time, even if it's just casually, in conversation, or as a way to commiserate with someone who is going through the same thing. For example, "Dude, I feel ya. I've been there myself and it fucking sucked ass." Then stop, mother fucker. Do not go on and on about it. If the other person wants to know more, they will fucking ask. This is not where you commandeer the conversation and make it all about you.

People hate that shit, especially if they've asked for your time to discuss what is on *their* mind. You can do a quid pro quo later: You bitch now, I bitch later. Bottom line: It's your shit, deal with it. Talk deeply with the trusted few or see Lesson 6 about paying for the services of a professional who is qualified to help people with such matters. Don't just let it stew around because you think your angst is alluring. Your angst doesn't make you an enigma, it makes you fucking annoying as shit.

Lesson 9: Put Your Money Where Your Mouth Is, Asshole

Stop fucking complaining and do something about it, or if you can't do something about it, try to find the good in the situation instead. Turn that fucking frown upside down, asshole,and make some fucking lemonade. There are problems everywhere: in your life, in other people's life, and the world so stop thinking that yours are the most important. There are bigger fucking fish to fry in this world than whether or not you look good in skinny jeans. If fitting into skinny jeans IS your biggest problem, then fucking do something about it. Stop going to Starbucks and buying fucking Salted Caramel Mocha Frappuccinos, (550 calories each, bitches) and do some cardio once in awhile with a few planks thrown in and that muffin top might disappear. Sitting around at Starbucks with your friends complaining about how jeans just don't look right on you, literally, isn't pretty. What is pretty? Someone who stops complaining, finds a fucking course of action, and without the permission of her stupid social circle, sets about solving the issues. Maybe once your ass looks good, you could turn your attention to more pressing matters, like the state of politics in America. I'm talking to you, Millennials Getting young people to use their considerable numbers and pressure to rise up against the shittyness that is going on in this country is going to change things around. Maybe if American politics was on your phone in an app or on Snapchat or in a stupid but catchy meme it would be more important than your vanity. Millennials outnumber Baby Boomers 83.1 million to 75.4 million, respectively, according to the Census Bureau, and those Boomers are going to be kicking off over the next few decades, if not all in one swoop. I'm not saying that Gen Xers or any other generation before yours is doing dick to try to change things but we don't have the numbers anymore. Millennials do. Mahatma Gandhi said "Be the fucking change you want to see in the world" but I'm pretty sure he left out the 'fucking' but the sentiment is the same. If you want the way things are to be different, then you have *to do* something about it. Demand something different. Demand change.

The first thing I suggest is to stop caring about celebrities and their stupid ass lives and antics. Nothing about them is real, it is all manufactured and even if it is real, who fucking cares? There is a huge industry that revolves around the periphery of what celebrities are doing, saying and wearing and it is completely meant to distract people from the more important matters of the day. "Oh, don't look at this horror over here and want to do something about it. Instead, look at this pretty shiny thing that sparkles! Preeetttyyy......" and then the horror is forgotten. Anyone pay attention in World History class? Anyone? Anyone? Bueller? Bueller? (If you are under the age of 40 and got that reference, I love you.) Does "bread and circuses" mean anything to you? If not, look it up. Right now. In your phone, the one that basically holds the entirety of human history, that gizmo in your hand, you know, the one you use to take endless fucking selfies? Even back in Rome, the main people of the day knew that if they placated the populace with cheap food and shitty entertainment, then they would be less likely to pay attention to what was actually going on around them and fucking do something about it. There might only be a handful of people in charge but what happens when you have thousand and thousands of people rising up against that handful? "Rising Up" doesn't necessarily mean taking up fucking arms and storming the damn castle. What it does mean is using your influence through what you are paying attention to and spending your money on to sway those in power around you to do what you need.

"But what can I do? I'm only one person...." You have money in your pocket, don't you? Money that maybe mommy and daddy gave you to spend because finding a job is just too hard? Where do you spend those dollars? What are you influencing through your spending? Think it doesn't matter? It does. Do you feel slightly pissed off about the Great Garbage Patches of the world? Oh wait, you don't know what the fuck those are? They are goddamn islands of trash that are floating around in the world's oceans because people don't recycle their shit, pick up their fucking trash and put in the proper receptacles, litter all over the fucking place, treating the land and oceans like fucking shit. The one in the Pacific Ocean covers more area than the size of Texas, twice. To give that some perspective, if you haven't done it and I suggest you do, driving across Texas takes about 13 hours, considering normal speeds and stops for supplies and gas. THIRTEEN FUCKING HOURS. Then consider that the Great Pacific Garbage Patch is twice that big. That's trash. Floating in the oceans, which are basically the Earth's lungs. Google Great Pacific Garbage Patch. Be appalled and then when you are done, rally your bros or your sisters and fucking do something about it. Stop buying bottled water, the bottles are rarely recycled. Recycle everything you can or better yet, just fucking stop buying stupid shit you don't need. The less you buy, the less you throw away. The less you throw away the less of it ends up in the ocean and in the belly of creatures who live on, in or near the ocean.

There is too much brilliance, talent and energy maturing into the world right now to waste it on stupid shit like celebrity reverence and personal vanity. You are all beautiful. You are. Just gorgeous. You don't need to take endless selfies and post them on Facebook to see how many likes they get to feel good about yourself. You also don't need to put your precious life in danger to get a selfie in some precarious location because you'll get a shit-ton of likes on Facebook. Facebook is NOT your life. Your life exists outside of your fucking phone.

Lesson 10: Put The Phone Down, Asshat

Remember in the last lesson when I said that in your hand you are holding a magnificent tiny machine that can reference the entirety of human existence and knowledge and it has the bonus of unlimited minutes, data and texting? You grew up with these damn things so they hardly seem miraculous but they are. If you handed an iPhone or an Android phone to me when I was 17, my teenage head would have fucking exploded. Dudes, we had a corded phone on the wall. If I wanted to talk on the phone, I had to sit in the kitchen. World knowledge was found in encyclopedias at the library or in the [gasp] Card Catalog. There was no texting. We fucking wrote letters! What? I know! Sounds fucking stupid, right? I'm telling you, you missed out on the whole passing notes thing in school. Now you just text each other and honestly it is *not* the same thing. The thrill of possibly getting caught, and if you did, the horror of having the note read in front of the class. Good times.

I'm not going to go so far as to say I walked to school uphill in the snow both directions, barefooted, year 'round but it does seem like each generation wants the next to know how much harder it was for them than you. In this case, this wondrous little gizmo is truly fucking fantastic. You have it in your hand constantly, why not use it for something good? Stop taking fucking pictures of yourself, we get it, you're pretty and you do amazeballs stuff, we don't care about what you are eating, just fucking eat it. We don't care about the macchiato you're about to consume and its cute little design in the froth. I'm sure it made you moist and you had a little orgasm while drinking it but we don't fucking care. We don't really need to know what you are doing every fucking minute of the day because in the end, you are accountable to no one anyway, right? Quit fucking checking in everywhere. "Aubrey just checked in at her Gynocologist."

WE DON'T CARE.

Just live your life without checking in. If people want to know where you are, I'm sure they will ask. I see hordes of young people walking all over town with their heads down, their noses in their phones, looking at things at don't matter. 99.7% of the things you are looking at in your phone don't matter. The fucking stupid games you play, the fucking pictures you take of stupid shit and the inane status updates on your social media are all unimportant. What is important is connecting with a fellow human being in real time, maybe the one that is right next to you, the one whose existence you haven't fucking acknowledged. Yeah, that guy. Look up long enough to see what is going on around you, right in front of you. The world. It exists outside your phone and it's pretty fucking cool and better than the one *in* your phone. Put your phone down. Better yet, turn the fucking thing off. Not on vibrate, not on mute, OFF. Turn it the fuck off. Put it in your car's glove box and walk away. Oh, God. That feels terrible, doesn't it? You're not connected to the inanity of life. You're looking. You're seeing. You're feeling real feelz right now. You see that? That is a person. A person you don't know. Go talk to them. With your mouth. Say words. Go do it. Right now. Good. Wait. Don't get in their windowless van, you stupid asshat. They offered you candy and a puppy? Are you fucking stupid?* Just kidding.

Seriously.

Talk to people. If you are in a meeting at work, you don't need to be live-tweeting how you are feeling about it. You need to put your phone down and give the people in the meeting with you your unflinching attention and respect. Pay attention, you doorknob.

Get used the the feeling of your hands without a phone in one of them. I'm as guilty as the next person is turning my car around to go home to get my phone. My reasoning is "What if I have an emergency?" This is not bad logic however I was driving for decades before cell phones were available at a reasonable price to the average person. I had a few fender benders or roadside emergencies and I managed to handle it and survive. Other people around you are also probably going to have their cell phones, too, so someone might stop and help you with that if you need it. I once owned an Isuzu I-Mark. That piece of shit blew a timing belt while I was driving on the outskirts of town, in the late afternoon. Not far from me was a house with a huge yard and a bunch of people having a lawn party. They were grilling out, playing games, having a good time. I just wandered over. Someone handed me a plate so that I could eat and asked me how I knew the hosts. I said that I didn't know the hosts and that my car broke down and I needed some help. Without missing a beat, a bunch of the men at the party went over to my car and stood around it with the hood up, some holding beers in that cross-armed sort of way, one poking around the engine. They came back and gave me their assessment then someone set about calling AAA for me. Of all the times I've broken down on the side of the road, and there have been a few, that was the nicest experience. There was no cell phone to use. I had to actually approach some strangers and ask them for help and what they gave me wasn't just help but hospitality. It was fantastic. People existed, the world existed, before cell phones and it was wonderful and still is.

Just recently, I went on a vacation and I was the only person with my particular cell phone carrier and I was so I ended up as the only one with no cell service all week. The first few days were weird. I kept checking the phone and there were no texts, no Facebook status to check, no calls to return. After a few days, I forgot where my phone was. I didn't need it for anything but check the time. I stopped checking the time because I didn't fucking care anymore. I was unplugged and it was fucking stupendous. This is something you need to do. Put the phone down and live your life for awhile without that little crack whore tweaking you every few minutes.

Don't pick up the phone at the movie theater. Don't be *that* asshole. If you are very important and you have very important business to attend to, then why the hell is your ass at the movies? Don't go or better yet, handle your business, turn the phone off and go on a date with your sweetie and enjoy the time with them. Don't text during a film, don't make a call. You are not that interesting. See Lesson 1. We don't care about your stupid shit, go back and re-read this lesson. People didn't pay the stupid price being charged for a movie to listen to your ass talk on the phone and ruin that shit. Same goes for your car. We don't think you are cool because of the music you are blaring. We think you are an inconsiderate idiot.

*For reals, don't get in vans or cars with people because they say they have candy or puppies, or a basket of kittens, or whatever else might entice you to do something stupid. This is all just to abduct your ass and do horrible things to it and then probably upload that shit to some sort of streaming online social media platform. Your life is that much harder now. This would be a bad decision, review Lesson 6.

Thanks for reading this book, now buy a copy for someone who needs this information. It is okay to let them know they are an asshole. What kind of friend would you be if you never said anything?